The Adventures of Captain Fearbeard

Ciaran Murtagh

Illustrated by Alex Paterson

Contents

OXFORD
UNIVERSITY PRESS

St Mary's RC Primary School
Park Drive
Bannockburn
Stirling
FK7 0EH
Tel: 01786 812294

Captain Fearbeard and the Mummy's Baby

Chapter 1
Packing the essentials

Captain Fearbeard's steely grey eyes shone with excitement as the bow of HMS *Albatross* sliced through the cool blue waters of the River Nile. When the mighty pyramid came into view the gentleman explorer clutched the rigging, slapped his thigh and turned to his cabin boy, Sam, in delight.

'There's adventure out there!' cried Fearbeard, sniffing the air. 'I can smell it!'

'I think that's my cheese and onion sandwich, sir,' said Sam, tucking his lunch back into his pocket. 'Sorry about that!'

'No matter!' said Fearbeard, his chin whiskers wafting majestically in the Egyptian breeze. 'Adventure often smells like a cheese and onion sandwich. Come! We must prepare for danger!'

Fearbeard stalked down the deck of the ship to his private quarters. Sam scurried close behind.

Captain Horatio Fearbeard was the bravest explorer in all of Queen Victoria's Empire. Ten-year-old Sam Lickspittle was, as Fearbeard so often told him, lucky enough to be his trusted cabin boy. Together they had braved the wailing weasels of Timbuktu, the vampire vipers of deepest darkest Borneo and the ninja grannies of Berwick-upon-Tweed.

Now they were about to embark on their most perilous adventure yet – a journey to the pyramids of Egypt in a quest for hidden treasure!

'Only pack the essentials,' ordered Fearbeard as Sam busied himself with a rucksack. 'Anti-poison

serum, a penknife and a packet of custard creams in case we stop for tea!'

Fearbeard loved custard cream biscuits almost as much as he loved adventure itself, and Sam dutifully shoved them into the bag. He was about to pack a book he'd been reading when Fearbeard stopped him. 'What's that?' asked Fearbeard. 'I said only pack the essentials!'

Sam showed him the book. 'It's about Ancient Egyptian hieroglyphs,' he explained. 'I thought it might come in useful.'

'We won't be needing that!' chuckled Fearbeard, tossing the book into a corner. 'Hieroglyphs indeed!'

5

Sam heaved the rucksack onto his shoulders and followed Fearbeard through the door. The River Nile shimmered in the sunlight as Fearbeard's ragtag crew assembled on the deck. Fearbeard gave them a smart salute and turned towards the gangplank.

'We'll be back with treasure by teatime!' he said, marching down the plank. 'No dawdling, Sam. Adventure awaits!'

Chapter 2
The tunnel of terror

On the banks of the Nile, Fearbeard gave a local guide a gold sovereign in return for two camels. Fearbeard huffed and puffed as he struggled to scramble onto the camel's back. Sam gave the Captain a shove and then nimbly hopped onto his own camel with ease.

'Nobody likes a show-off,' mumbled Fearbeard, the heat of the Egyptian sun making his whiskers wilt. 'I think your camel's angry with you,' he said.

'Why do you say that?' asked Sam.

'Because he's got the hump!' laughed Fearbeard, slapping his thigh with delight. 'The *hump*! Get it? Because he's a camel!'

Sam laughed along. He always found it best to laugh at Fearbeard's terrible jokes rather than suffer the terrible sulk that followed if he didn't.

When they arrived at the entrance to the pyramid, the guide helped them both down and Fearbeard studied the tunnel opening with an expert eye.

'I warn you!' said the guide. 'Do not enter this pyramid. It is cursed!'

Fearbeard's eyes narrowed. 'My good sir!' he snarled. 'I am Captain Horatio Fearbeard. I have tackled the sucking squid of the San Sebastian straits, the rampaging rhinos of Rajastan and the killer kittens of Kathmandu! Your curse does not scare me!'

The guide backed away as Sam peered into the gloom. 'If we're going in there, sir,' he said, 'we'll need some flaming torches.'

'Sam!' snapped Fearbeard. 'Watch your language!'

'No,' explained Sam, producing two long sticks from his rucksack and lighting them with a match. 'Flaming torches!'

'Oh yes,' mumbled Fearbeard. 'I knew that!'

Sam handed one of the torches to Fearbeard and together they set off into the darkness. Their footsteps crunched on the sandy floor and their flickering flames cast strange shadows across the tunnel walls.

'There could be anything lurking in here,' said Fearbeard as they walked. 'Giant spiders ... '

Sam felt a shiver run down his spine.

'Vampire bats ... '

Sam tried not to listen.

'Zombie cockroaches with fangs as long as your arm!'

'Could you stop that, sir?' snapped Sam. He had heard enough.

'Just trying to lighten the mood,' said Fearbeard with a shrug. 'Some people are sooooo touchy! Ooh, what's this?'

Fearbeard had stopped. A lever protruded from the stone wall by his shoulder.

'Don't touch that, sir!' said Sam. 'These pyramids are riddled with booby traps!'

'Stuff and nonsense,' said Fearbeard, yanking the lever. 'I might have won a prize!'

Suddenly, wind howled down the tunnel
and a loud rumbling filled the air.

'What do you think I've won?'
asked Fearbeard, rubbing his hands
together in delight.

'A giant boulder, sir!' shouted Sam.

'No!' huffed Fearbeard. 'That
would be a rubbish prize!'

'No, sir!' said Sam, pointing up the
tunnel. 'A giant boulder! Run!'

Fearbeard's eyes grew wide with
terror as a massive rock rolled down the
tunnel. If it hit them, they'd be crushed to
death for sure! Sam grabbed Fearbeard's arm
and together they ran for their lives. They dodged
left and right, taking one tunnel after another in
a frantic race to escape. Wherever they ran, the
boulder followed. Desperate, Fearbeard yanked
Sam into an opening.

'Oh dear,' said Fearbeard, stopping dead in
his tracks.

'What is it?' asked Sam.

Fearbeard pointed. 'Dead end!'

Sam's heart sank. The boulder was closing in on them. There was no escape.

'Don't worry,' said Fearbeard. 'I'll think of something!'

Sam waited while the Captain rubbed his beard, deep in concentration.

'I've got it!' said Fearbeard with a triumphant smile. 'I need a custard cream!'

Sam was confused. 'How will that help?'

'If I'm dying, I'm dying happy!' explained Fearbeard.

'This is no time for a custard cream, sir!' spluttered Sam, frantically searching for a way out.

'Spoilsport!' grumbled Fearbeard, slumping to the floor.

The boulder rumbled towards them. Sam tapped the walls and tested the bricks but nothing moved.

'Hang on!' said Fearbeard. 'What's this?'

Sam looked. Down on the ground, Fearbeard had found another lever.

'Pull it!' ordered Sam. The boulder was only inches away.

'Hold your horses, m'boy!' said Fearbeard. 'You know what happened last time!' He pointed at the boulder.

'With the greatest respect, sir,' shouted Sam, 'what have we got to lose?'

Fearbeard nodded and yanked the lever. To their surprise the left-hand wall slid open.

'A secret passage!' exclaimed Sam. 'Quick!'

Sam pushed Fearbeard through the gap and

jumped in after him as the boulder rolled past.

'I saved the day again!' laughed Fearbeard. '*Now* can I have a custard cream?'

Sam was about to explain that the day wouldn't have needed saving if Fearbeard had left the lever alone in the first place, when he gasped at the sight that lay behind Fearbeard's shoulder. 'A burial chamber!' he said.

Fearbeard turned to look. 'My, my, my! Would you believe it? I've done it again!'

The room on the other side of the secret passage was filled with treasure, and at the heart of it all was a solid gold sarcophagus covered in jewels and mysterious hieroglyphs.

'How are we going to get this lot back to the ship?' said Sam.

'My dear boy,' chuckled Fearbeard, plonking himself down on a golden throne. '*We* are not. *You* are! I'll hold the flaming torches while you get busy. Start with the sarcophagus!'

Sam's heart sank as he looked at the sarcophagus and the piles of treasure. This was going to take ages.

Chapter 3
The sarcophagus struggle

Captain Fearbeard sat in a deckchair watching Sam drag the jewelled sarcophagus up the gangplank.

'Put your back into it, m'lad!' instructed Fearbeard, reclining in the deckchair and sipping a cup of Earl Grey tea.

Sam shot Fearbeard an angry stare. 'It would be much quicker if you leant a hand,' he wheezed.

'No can do, old chap!' sighed Fearbeard sadly. 'I've used my hands too much already today. Don't want to wear them out!'

Sam pulled the sarcophagus across the deck and into Fearbeard's private quarters. It weighed a ton and left long scratch marks all over the bow.

It had taken much of the afternoon to get the sarcophagus out of the pyramid and back to HMS *Albatross*. It would have been much quicker if Captain Fearbeard, who 'was sure he knew the way', hadn't got lost for three hours in the pyramid's maze-like tunnels.

Sam pushed the sarcophagus up against Fearbeard's desk and sank, exhausted, to the floor.

'No time for napping, old bean!' called Fearbeard from the door. 'You've got another twenty trips to do before the tomb is empty.'

Sam pointed at the sun setting through the porthole. 'It'll be dark soon, sir!' he panted. 'Can't we, I mean *I*, get the rest in the morning?'

'I suppose so,' said Fearbeard with a nod. 'Besides, we've got the best bit!' He tapped the sarcophagus. 'And we don't want you missing out on the celebration banquet, do we?'

Captain Fearbeard always celebrated his achievements with a slap-up banquet – it was tradition!

'I wonder what we're having,' he said, calling

towards the kitchen. 'Chef! What's for dinner?'

Chef McStain, the portly ship's cook, stuck his head out of the kitchen door. 'Chicken feet in orange sauce,' he growled.

Fearbeard wrinkled his nose. 'Sounds disgusting!' he spat. 'Anything else?'

Chef thought for a moment. 'Poulet à l'orange!' he offered.

'Perfect!' said Fearbeard with a grin. 'Sounds much better!'

Fearbeard closed the door and looked at the sarcophagus with greedy eyes. 'It must be worth a fortune,' he said, examining the rubies and sapphires that covered the lid. 'I'll wager there's loads more treasure inside!'

'I doubt it, sir,' said Sam. 'Sarcophagi usually contain a mummy.'

'Don't be ridiculous!' said Fearbeard, running his hand along the edge of the casket. 'Who'd leave their mummy in there? I left mine in a home by the sea. She loves it! Cribbage on Tuesdays, bridge on Thursdays and on Saturdays they get to play a concertina!'

'Not that sort of mummy,' explained Sam, retrieving his book on Ancient Egypt from the corner where Fearbeard had thrown it. 'Look!'

Sam pointed to an illustration of a sarcophagus identical to the one lying in the Captain's quarters. When he turned the page, a picture of a mummy wrapped in bandages stared back at them.

'Stuff and nonsense!' said Fearbeard. 'Ah! Here's what I've been looking for!' He ran his finger over a catch hidden in the lid of the sarcophagus and the top creaked open. Dust billowed into the room and a strange musty smell filled the air. Fearbeard rubbed his hands together with glee and peered into the casket.

'Oh,' he sighed with disappointment. 'It seems you were right. No treasure, just a stinky old mummy.'

Fearbeard closed the lid with a thud. 'It can stay here until morning,' he said. 'Then we'll, I mean *you'll*, put it in the hold.'

Fearbeard stepped out onto the deck, leaving Sam alone with the sarcophagus. The hieroglyphs seemed to sparkle in the candlelight. Curious, Sam flipped open his book and began to translate.

'Star, scarab, lion and owl,' he muttered, scanning the page for clues. 'Here lies the tomb of the Pharaoh Queen's Mummy,' he translated. 'Cursed for all eternity!'

Sam put down his book and shivered. The guide had warned them about the curse and Fearbeard hadn't listened. Now the cursed sarcophagus was on their ship!

Sam examined the hieroglyphs some more. Serpent, arm, squiggle, stone. 'The curse comes to pass every full moon,' translated Sam. He breathed a sigh of relief – they were safe unless tonight was a full moon, and that was very unlikely.

Sam was about to go and lay the table for dinner when he heard Fearbeard's voice booming through the porthole window. 'What a lovely night, boys!' declared the Captain to no one in particular. 'And would you look at that! A full moon!'

Sam dropped the book in surprise. He had a very bad feeling in the pit of his stomach which, for once, had nothing to do with Chef's cooking!

Chapter 4
A rude awakening

With the crew assembled in the dining room, Chef McStain ladled his poulet à l'orange onto a plate and handed it to Sam. Sam stared at the meal. Two chicken feet stuck out of a pool of orange gunk. He shook his head – Chef McStain's cooking was getting worse.

'Be careful, Sam,' sniggered Fearbeard, pointing at the chicken feet. 'It looks like your food might have a bit of a kick!'

Sam smiled dutifully and prodded the food with a fork.

The six members of the HMS *Albatross* crew were gathered around an oak table. Alongside Fearbeard and Sam sat midshipman Trevor Bunion; John Pilchard, the ship's red-headed first mate; and Pat Leotard, chief rigging climber. Chef McStain gave himself an extra large portion and sat down to join them.

The food looked even more disgusting than usual, but it wasn't the yucky chicken that was stopping Sam from eating. The prospect of a cursed Egyptian mummy didn't leave him with much of an appetite.

Sam had tried to warn Fearbeard about the curse but he hadn't listened. Sam had even offered to drag the sarcophagus off the ship, but Fearbeard had waved his concerns away as if swatting a fly.

As the rest of the crew were eating, a strange moaning, gurgling sound filled the air. Sam froze in terror. Was the mummy on the move so soon?

John Pilchard smiled apologetically to his shipmates and patted his tummy. 'Sorry,' he said, his cheeks glowing red. 'I ate that a bit too fast!'

The crew returned to their supper but suddenly the strange gurgling sound came again, louder this time. All eyes turned to John Pilchard once more.

'Hey!' he spluttered. 'That one wasn't me!'

Pat Leotard raised a hand. 'I think it was me that time!' he admitted.

Sam wasn't sure the noise was any of his shipmates' tummies. It sounded more like the menacing moan of a malevolent mummy, but before he had a chance to say anything, Fearbeard clattered his fork onto the plate in anger. 'Honestly!' he fumed. 'It's like eating with a herd of Siberian buffalo! Don't you lot have *any* manners?'

Just then, the bandaged face of the mummy appeared at the porthole behind Fearbeard. Sam's mouth fell open in shock.

'This is exactly what I'm talking about!' spluttered Fearbeard, nodding at Sam in disgust. 'You're all belching and Sam's chewing with his mouth open! Where are your manners?'

Sam closed his mouth as the mummy stuck its face through the open porthole. A pair of eyes glowed red among the dirty, dusty bandages. In terror, Sam pointed at the porthole.

'And now he's pointing at me!' bellowed Fearbeard. 'How rude can you get?'

'M ... m ... m ... ' stammered Sam, pointing at the mummy in the porthole.

'Spit it out, boy!' demanded Fearbeard, but Sam was too scared to speak.

Meanwhile, the rest of the crew had seen what Sam was pointing at and were slowly getting up from their seats. John Pilchard edged towards the door.

'And where do you think you're going, Mr Pilchard?' huffed Fearbeard. 'You're supposed to *ask* before you leave the table.'

'Mummy!' spluttered Pilchard, pointing at the porthole. 'Mummy!'

'It's no use crying for your mummy now!' snapped Fearbeard. 'She's not going to help you, is she?'

Chef McStain picked up a bread roll and threw it at the porthole. The roll missed and bounced off Captain Fearbeard's nose.

'Have you all gone completely mad?' shouted Fearbeard, dodging another bread roll, then another and another, each one thrown by a member of the HMS *Albatross* crew.

'That! Is! It!' roared Fearbeard, picking himself up off the floor. 'You are all confined to quarters forever!'

The mummy reached a bandaged arm through the porthole and tapped Fearbeard on the shoulder.

'For goodness' sake,' said Fearbeard, turning to see who was bothering him. 'Don't you know it's rude to interrupt a ... '

Fearbeard's words stuck in his throat as he stared into the blazing red eyes of the mummy. 'Mummy!' he shrieked. 'Mummy!'

The mummy grabbed Fearbeard's collar and hauled herself through the window. The crew ran for their lives. Fearbeard shook the mummy loose and scampered under the table. Sam dived under to join him.

'What are you doing, sir?' asked Sam. 'You're not scared are you?'

'Me?' spluttered Fearbeard indignantly. 'Scared? Of course not! I was just ... erm ... erm ... conducting a surprise cobweb inspection.'

The mummy thrust a bandaged hand under the table and tweaked Fearbeard's nose.

'Well, if you've quite finished your cobweb inspection, sir,' said Sam, 'I think we need to get out of here!'

'Good idea,' said Fearbeard. 'I was just about to suggest that!'

Sam and Fearbeard crawled under the table towards the door and then ran out across the deck. When the mummy saw them she gave chase.

'Believe in the curse yet?' asked Sam as they ran.

'Nobody likes a smarty-pants, Sam,' said Fearbeard, dodging around the mast.

On the other side of the ship, the door to the Captain's private quarters was swinging open. 'Quick!' said Sam. 'Hide!'

Sam led the Captain into his room and slammed the door shut. In the cabin, the lid to the sarcophagus was open and four pairs of eyes peered out at them from behind the Captain's desk.

'What are you lot doing here?' snapped Fearbeard as the crew emerged sheepishly from their hiding place. 'These are my *private* quarters. We will have to have a serious talk about boundaries!'

Behind them the mummy was shoulder-barging the door. Sam dragged across a chair and wedged it under the handle.

'It won't keep her out for long!' said Sam, his eyes falling on the open sarcophagus. The hieroglyphs still sparkled in the candlelight. Sam pulled his book from his pocket and began to search for the right page.

'This is no time for a bedtime story, Sam!' snapped Fearbeard. 'In case you hadn't noticed, we're under attack from a killer mummy!'

'This isn't a storybook,' explained Sam patiently. 'It translates hieroglyphs. A clue to how to stop the curse might be on the sarcophagus!'

'Well, why didn't you mention this amazing book sooner?' huffed Fearbeard.

'I did!' snapped Sam, but realizing there was no time to argue, he ran to the sarcophagus and began to translate the rest of the hieroglyphs.

'It says,' began Sam, 'that the Pharaoh Queen lost her baby one night long ago. As punishment for her carelessness she was cursed to spend every full moon searching for it, even after death!'

Fearbeard and the crew gasped in surprise.

'The mummy Queen,' continued Sam, 'will kill anyone who stands in her way.'

The crew gasped again. Behind them the door began to splinter as the mummy pounded it with her fist.

'So how do we stop her?' asked Fearbeard.

Sam scratched his head. The hieroglyphs didn't say, but an idea leapt into his mind. 'What if the mummy finds her baby?' he asked.

'Then she'll stop looking,' said Trevor Bunion with a nod.

'Which means we'll be safe,' agreed John Pilchard.

'But there is no mummy's baby!' snapped Fearbeard. 'This is a ridiculous conversation!'

Sam's eyes sparkled mischievously. 'The mummy doesn't have to find her *real* baby,' he said. 'We just have to make her think that she has. I'll do it! It's a dangerous plan, but it might just work.'

'Hang on!' said Fearbeard, arching an eyebrow. 'Did you say danger? If there's danger afoot then I, Captain Fearbeard, shall do it!'

'Are you sure you want to, sir?' asked Sam.

'Of course!' said Fearbeard with a smile. 'I'd do anything for this ship. Now what's the plan?'

Sam turned to the crew. 'Fetch me every loo roll in the cabin,' he ordered. 'Quickly!'

Fearbeard's face fell. 'Not my extra-soft secret stash?' he begged.

'Even the extra-soft secret stash,' said Sam. 'We're going to make a mummy's baby!'

Chapter 5
All wrapped up

Sam wrapped the last of the loo roll around Captain
Fearbeard's face and tied it with a knot.

'If I'd known this was your brilliant plan,' said
Fearbeard, his voice muffled behind fifteen rolls
of toilet tissue, 'you could have done it yourself!'

The cabin door splintered as the mummy
barged against it. A bandaged arm appeared
through the cracked wood and fumbled for the
chair. Sam looked at Captain Fearbeard. He was
covered from head to toe in loo roll. All you could
see of his face were two angry grey eyes and a few
wayward beard hairs.

'He looks good to me!' said Chef McStain,

appraising his work.

'Aye!' agreed John Pilchard. 'Just like a mummy's baby!'

'One last thing,' said Sam, rummaging in his backpack and producing a dummy. 'You'll need this!'

'I am not sucking mmmtht!' spluttered Fearbeard as Sam wedged the dummy into the Captain's bandaged mouth.

'Where did that come from?' asked Trevor Bunion.

'It was the only thing I had with me when I was found,' explained Sam. 'I've kept it ever since.'

Sam Lickspittle was an orphan. Captain Fearbeard had taken him on as a cabin boy as a favour to the orphanage's fearsome owner, Clint Leatherstrap. Captain Fearbeard's adventures may have been dangerous, but they were a walk in the park compared to Clint Leatherstrap's bullying ways.

Behind them the mummy pushed the chair out of her way.

'She's coming in!' said Sam. 'Ready, Captain?'

'Mmmth! Mmmth! Mmmth!' said the Captain.

'I'll take that as a yes,' said Sam.

The door flew open and the mummy stood framed in the doorway, her red eyes blazing. She lurched towards the crew and they all took a step back, leaving the mummified Fearbeard all alone in the centre of the room.

When the mummy saw the bandaged Captain she stumbled towards him. Fearbeard shot his crew a terrified look and began to whimper. The mummy stretched out a hand. Fearbeard closed his eyes. But instead of choking him to death with her mighty strength, the mummy gave Fearbeard a tender stroke on the chin.

'Brilliant!' hissed Sam. 'She thinks you sound like a baby!'

'That's because he usually does!' sniggered Trevor Bunion quietly under his breath.

Captain Fearbeard whimpered even louder and the mummy patted him on the head. Then she picked up the chair she had knocked over and sat down. When she was comfortable she picked up Fearbeard and plonked him onto her lap, bending him forward and giving him a mighty slap on the back.

Fearbeard's dummy shot out of his mouth and flew across the room.

'What's she doing?' he spluttered.

'I think she's burping you,' said Trevor, going a little gooey eyed. 'Ain't that cute!'

The mummy gave Fearbeard another fierce slap.

'But I don't need a BUUURRRRP!' spluttered Fearbeard, letting out a belch so loud it rattled the fillings in Trevor Bunion's teeth.

Satisfied, the mummy stopped slapping Fearbeard and gave him a clothy kiss.

'She stinks!' said Fearbeard, sticking out his tongue in disgust.

'Just play along,' insisted Sam, 'and we might live until the morning!'

The mummy opened her mouth and the weirdest sound any of them had ever heard filled the room. It was somewhere between a cat crying and a train whistle.

'What's she doing now?' asked Pat Leotard, sticking his fingers in his ears.

'I think she's singing him a lullaby,' said
John Pilchard, wiping away a soppy tear. 'Isn't
she lovely?'

The mummy rocked Fearbeard back and forth
on her lap as she sang her tuneless song.

'Come on,' said Sam quietly, leading his
shipmates out of the room. 'Let's leave them to it.'

'Hey!' shouted Fearbeard over the horrendous noise. 'Where are you lot going?'

'There's a banquet to be eaten,' said Chef McStain with a sniff. 'I didn't slave over a hot stove all day for nothing!'

'But what about me?' said Fearbeard as the mummy tickled him under the chin.

'Stay here all night,' explained Sam. 'The mummy will get back into the sarcophagus when the full moon goes down and you'll be free!'

'All night!' spluttered Fearbeard. 'In this smell? With that racket?'

Sam gave Captain Fearbeard a smart salute. 'Well done, Captain,' he said proudly. 'You've saved the day again!'

Fearbeard smiled to himself as Sam closed the door. 'You know,' he said quietly, 'I think he might be right.'

Back in the dining hall Chef McStain divided the Captain's portion of food between the rest of the men as the terrible song of the mummy drifted across the deck.

Chapter 6
Sarcopha-gone

The following morning Sam sat on the bow of
the *Albatross* and carefully unravelled Captain
Fearbeard. The moon had sunk some time ago,
and when it had completely disappeared behind
the pyramid the mummy had released the Captain,
returned to her sarcophagus and closed the lid.

'Well, Sam,' said Fearbeard as the last of the toilet
tissue fell to the floor. 'We've no loo paper, that
terrible singing made my earwax melt, I didn't get a
wink of sleep and I stink of dirty old bandages, but
most importantly I saved the day!'

'I couldn't agree more, sir,' said Sam, picking bits
of loo paper off the Captain's face.

Sam watched the crew heave the sarcophagus
back down the gangplank towards the pyramid.
Captain Fearbeard had decided to leave the mummy
guarding her treasure rather than risk another
wailing lullaby on the journey home. When the
crew returned they were ready to set sail.

'Weigh anchor!' called Fearbeard.

'It's very heavy, sir,' answered John Pilchard.

'That's not what I meant!' snapped Fearbeard. 'Oh never mind, just get on with it!'

The men heaved the anchor onto the deck of the *Albatross* and the strong Egyptian wind filled the ship's sails as Trevor Bunion guided her into fast-flowing waters. As they sailed from the banks of the Nile, Fearbeard called Sam to his side and together they stood shoulder to shoulder as the horizon heaved into view.

'Onward to adventure, Sam!' said Fearbeard. 'Who knows what daring deeds and brave escapades we will face next time.'

'Must there be a next time, Captain?' asked Sam.

'Invariably!' crowed Fearbeard with a grin. 'Invariably!'

HMS *Albatross* and her crew floated down the Nile towards adventures new, leaving the mummy to her rest and Fearbeard and Sam arguing over whose turn it was to do the washing up.

Captain Fearbeard in Never Forget a Yeti

Chapter 1
A lot of hot air

Captain Fearbeard clutched the side of the wicker basket as the hot-air balloon sailed through the sky. At his side, cabin boy Sam Lickspittle shivered in the icy wind. Clouds floated beneath them and the barren wilderness of the snowy Arctic stretched far below the balloon like a soft white blanket.

'There's adventure out there,' said Fearbeard, sniffing the air excitedly. 'I can smell it!'

'I think that might be my lunch,' said Sam, cracking his teeth on a frozen sandwich. 'Pickled tuna today.'

'Adventure often smells like a pickled tuna sandwich!' announced Fearbeard, casually tossing another sandbag over the side of the balloon. The balloon rose a little and sailed on. Sam and Fearbeard were on the trail of the mythical Arctic yeti in their chilliest adventure yet!

As the hot-air balloon gained height,
Fearbeard's breath hung in the air like tiny clouds
and icicles hung from his whiskers. They had
abandoned their ship and crew when frozen ice
had stopped the *Albatross* sailing any further.

Fearbeard wasn't the kind of man to let a little
ice stop him, so he and Sam were journeying on in
the emergency hot-air balloon Fearbeard kept for
such occasions. He was determined to capture a
real live yeti and bring it back to London Zoo so
that Queen Victoria would give him a medal.

'Do you even know what a yeti looks like?'
asked Sam as they floated over snowdrifts
and glaciers.

'I have mauled the moaning mosquitoes of Mozambique,' said Captain Fearbeard, 'the poisonous puffer fish of the Peru peninsula and the terrifying tadpoles of Tanzania! Of course I know what a yeti looks like!'

'So what does it look like, then?' asked Sam.

Fearbeard's eyes shifted from side to side. 'They're hairy,' he said finally. 'And they've got teeth and eyes and things ... Pass me a custard cream, there's a good boy!'

Sam rummaged in his rucksack and tossed a biscuit to the Captain. He was beginning to think that, just like the balloon they were sailing in, Fearbeard was full of hot air!

The cabin boy pulled his scarf a little tighter around his neck, rubbed his hands together and dreamed of the warm fire waiting for him back on the *Albatross*. His daydream was rudely interrupted by a shout from Fearbeard.

'Mountains!' spluttered the Captain, pointing to the horizon. 'Hundreds of them!'

In the distance a range of enormous mountains loomed into view. They were flying too low to get over the first peak. If they didn't get higher quickly they were sure to crash.

'More height!' ordered Fearbeard. 'Quick!'

Sam was way ahead of the Captain and had already begun to untie all of the sandbags from the side of the balloon, dropping them onto the snowy ground below. The balloon rose a little, but it was nowhere near enough. They were going to hit the first mountain they came to.

'We need to lose more weight!' shouted Sam.

'Speak for yourself,' said Fearbeard, patting his tummy.

'No,' explained Sam. 'We need to lose weight from the balloon if we don't want to crash!'

The mountains were getting closer by the second. Sam scoured the basket for something to throw out. The Captain's trunk lay in the corner. Sam flipped it open and searched through the contents.

'We don't need these!' he said, picking up a bag of marbles and preparing to throw them overboard.

Fearbeard stopped him. 'I can't lose my

marbles!' he spluttered. 'They're my lucky set!'

'Some might say you lost your marbles a long time ago,' muttered Sam under his breath. 'What about this?'

Sam was holding a battered garden gnome.

Fearbeard snatched the gnome out of his hands and clutched him to his chest. 'Colin's been in the family for generations,' he said. 'Where he goes, I go!'

'Then you can both go overboard,' mumbled Sam as the mountain loomed ever closer.

'Why is it my stuff that has to go, anyway?' said Fearbeard, slamming the lid of his trunk shut and sitting on it like a petulant schoolboy. 'What have you got to chuck?'

Sam tipped his tiny rucksack onto the wicker floor and rifled through the contents. 'There's a gold sovereign,' he said.

'Over the side!' ordered Fearbeard.

Reluctantly, Sam did as he was told.

'And look!' said Fearbeard, pointing at the floor. 'There's a penknife. That can go too!'

'But sir ... ' protested Sam.

Fearbeard held up a finger. 'An adventurer's life is full of sacrifices,' he snapped.

Obediently Sam threw the penknife into the snow. Despite his sacrifices the hot-air balloon wasn't getting any higher and the mountain was getting closer and closer. Sam felt in his pockets for anything else he could throw. His fingers clasped around his pea-shooter.

He was about to throw it over the side when Fearbeard stopped him. 'That won't be enough, Sam,' said Fearbeard, giving him a grave look.

'The only way we're going to get over that mountain top is for one of us to make the ultimate sacrifice!'

'You mean jump, sir?' spluttered Sam.

Fearbeard nodded.

'I can't ask you to do that!' said Sam.

'Of course you can't,' said Fearbeard with a sympathetic smile. 'But I can ask *you* to do it! I'm Captain after all!'

Sam couldn't believe his ears. 'You want me to jump!' he gasped.

'You'll be fine,' said Fearbeard. 'It's snow. It's known for being soft! I'll pick you up on the way back.'

Sam wasn't so sure. The snow looked a lot like ice to him. Fearbeard pushed him towards the side of the basket. The mountain was so close that Sam felt like he could reach out and touch it. Just as the brave cabin boy was preparing to launch himself into the unknown, Fearbeard and Sam were flung to the floor by a mighty gust of wind. It blew the balloon clear of the mountain top and down into the plateau beyond.

'That was close,' said Fearbeard, dusting himself down. 'Next time pack a bit more lightly!'

Sam was thinking how hard it would be to shove Colin the garden gnome up the Captain's nose when Fearbeard pointed towards the ground.

'Footprints!' he cheered. 'I've done it again! We're on the trail of the yeti now, m'boy!'

Below them, footprints stretched into the distance. They were big and deep and looked like they belonged to something very unpleasant indeed.

'Isn't this exciting!' said Fearbeard.

Sam shook his head. He wasn't sure *exciting* was the word he would use – *terrifying* seemed much more appropriate.

Chapter 2
Winter wonderland

Safely over the mountain, Fearbeard landed the
hot-air balloon in the soft white snow of the
plateau. He fastened the balloon to a boulder with a
length of rope and took a large sack from his
trunk. He stuffed the sack inside his jacket then
knelt down to examine the trail of footprints.
Each of the footprints was much bigger than a
human foot, with four toes instead of five, each
ending in a sharp claw.

'Those are yeti footprints all right,' said
Fearbeard, nodding sagely. 'We just need to follow
them and Bob's your uncle – or should that be yeti?'

Fearbeard chuckled and set off across the plateau.
Sam scampered to keep up and soon the pair of
adventurers were trudging through the snow at a
brisk pace.

'Did you bring the custard creams?' asked
Fearbeard as they walked.

Sam delved into his rucksack and produced the
packet. He passed it to Fearbeard and the Captain

shoved two biscuits in his mouth. 'To keep my strength up!' he explained through a shower of biscuit crumbs.

They were following the footprints up a steep slope into the heart of the mountains. The sun, although high in the sky, gave off no heat and the snowy wilderness stretched as far as the eye could see. Fearbeard chomped down on another biscuit. The sound echoed all around. Up ahead the noise dislodged a sheet of snow and it tumbled down the mountain in a ferocious avalanche.

Sam held Fearbeard back as the snow settled. 'Perhaps that's enough custard creams for now, sir,' he said, taking back the packet.

Fearbeard and Sam followed the footprints towards the snowfall.

'Yetis don't eat custard creams you know,' said the Captain as they walked, a playful smile on his lips. 'What do you think they like as a treat?'

Sam shrugged. He had no idea.

'Ice-burgers!' spluttered Fearbeard, slapping his thigh in delight. 'They like *ice-* burgers!'

Fearbeard collapsed into a fit of giggles and Sam

chuckled along. By the Captain's standards that
was a pretty good joke.

Suddenly Fearbeard stopped walking.

'What's the matter?' asked Sam.

They had reached the top of the slope where the
Captain's custard cream avalanche had covered the
ground. The snowfall had hidden the footprints
and what was more, they were at a fork in the road.
Which was the right path to take? Without the
footprints to guide them, there was no way to tell.

'Which way?' asked Sam.

Fearbeard licked his finger and held it up to
test the wind. He quietly did some calculations,
scratched his head, fluffed his beard and then
turned to Sam.

'I have absolutely no idea!' he announced with a
sheepish smile.

'That's just perfect,' said Sam, crossing his arms in a huff. 'What now?'

Fearbeard looked at the two paths. 'Eeeny meeny?' he offered hopefully.

Suddenly, a strange rumbling sound filled the air. It was coming from the left-hand path.

'Sounds like a yeti to me!' said Fearbeard confidently. 'This way!'

Sam followed Fearbeard along the left-hand path and up a hill. The sound got louder and louder until it seemed to come from all around them.

As they turned the corner, Sam stopped dead in his tracks. Up ahead, lying in the entrance to a cave, a strange creature was snoring its head off. The creature was twice the size of Captain Fearbeard. It was covered from shaggy head to shaggy toe in thick white fur and it was fast asleep. Sam was sure that he and the Captain had just found their first yeti.

'See,' said Captain Fearbeard, taking in the sight. 'Hair, teeth, eyes! Just like I described!'

Sam also noticed the razor-sharp claws and the

fangs that the Captain had failed to mention.

'Go on then!' said Fearbeard, pushing him towards the sleeping creature. 'Wake him up!'

Sam could hardly believe his ears. There was an old saying that Fearbeard was fond of quoting. It went: 'Let sleeping dogs lie.' Sam was sure it applied to yetis too.

'Why would I want to wake him up, sir?' he asked.

'So he can walk back to the balloon with us,' explained Fearbeard. 'How else are we going to get him home? Carry him?'

The Captain took the sack from inside his jacket. 'Don't worry,' he said. 'We'll catch him in this. I bet he's just like a big cuddly teddy bear!'

'I bet he's not,' said Sam, tentatively making his way towards the cave entrance and the sleeping, drooling yeti.

Chapter 3
The human alarm clock

As Sam tiptoed towards the snoring yeti a shiver ran down his spine that had nothing to do with the icy weather. The yeti was huge and his skewer-like claws glinted in the Arctic sun. The cave was obviously the yeti's home and bits of bone and fur littered the entrance. Sam hoped that he and Fearbeard weren't about to join the pile of leftovers.

He was only a few metres away when the yeti sniffed the air and yawned. Sam froze. For a moment the yeti's cavernous mouth opened to reveal row upon row of sharp yellow teeth. Slime dripped from the end of one of the fangs and melted a small hole in the ice. Sam held his breath until the creature closed his mouth and started snoring once again.

Further back, Fearbeard was cowering behind a boulder, cloth sack at the ready. 'Go on!' he said, ushering Sam forward with a wave. 'He won't bite ... probably!'

Sam took another step. He was now face to face with the yeti. He could feel its rancid breath on his face – it stank of rotting fish and mouldy bread. The yeti's snoring was like the growl of a mountain lion. Even though it made Sam's ears throb he was glad it was there – the moment the snoring stopped it meant the yeti was awake and Sam was in serious trouble.

Sam had no idea how to wake a yeti. When Fearbeard wanted to wake up Sam, he usually tickled his toes. Perhaps the same thing worked for ice monsters. He bent down and tickled the massive furry foot of the yeti. The foot was the size of Sam's arm and it was covered in thick padded skin.

For a moment the yeti stopped snoring and licked its lips. Sam backed away. But instead of waking up, the yeti reached down and gave his foot a scratch with a talon-like finger.

As the yeti returned to his snoring, Sam searched around for something else he could use to wake it up. His eyes came to rest on a long purple feather lying in the snow. Sam picked it up and stretched it towards the yeti's big black nose. He tickled the yeti's nostril with the tip of the feather and waited.

The yeti wrinkled his nose, opened his mouth and did the loudest sneeze Sam had ever heard. He was knocked onto his back by the force of the wind and found himself splattered by disgusting green gloop.

'That is *snot* what you wanted to happen!' giggled Fearbeard from behind his boulder.

Sam ignored Fearbeard and wiped the yeti's nose slime from his shoulder. This was getting annoying. It was time to try something that was sure to wake it up. He clambered up the yeti's body towards its snoring face. The yeti had two furry ears on the top of his head. Tentatively, Sam lifted one with his finger, took a deep breath and shouted into the yeti's ear. 'Wakey-wakey, Mr Yeti!' he bellowed.

The yeti didn't even flinch. Sam couldn't believe it.

'Wakey-wakey, Mr Yeti!' he shouted again.

This time the sleeping yeti batted Sam away with a lazy arm and he tumbled to the ground, landing with a splat in the snow. Nothing was working. If shouting and tickling didn't wake the yeti, what would?

Suddenly a massive snowball whistled past Sam's ear and smashed into the cave roof above the snoring monster. Where had that come from? Sam turned to look and saw Fearbeard eagerly scooping up another armful of snow.

'Duck!' commanded Fearbeard as he let rip with the second snowball.

Sam dived out of the way as the snowball splatted into the yeti's face.

Fearbeard punched the air in triumph. 'Bullseye!' he shouted. 'Fearbeard does it again!'

Sam was about to suggest to Fearbeard that throwing snowballs at a yeti wasn't the brightest idea he'd ever had when he noticed something. The snoring had stopped.

Sam's heart began to thump. He turned to look at the yeti and found a pair of yellow eyes staring back at him. The yeti stamped his foot in anger and the ice beneath them began to crack.

'Well that's broken the ice!' chuckled Fearbeard.

'I see that, Captain,' said Sam, very quietly backing away.

The yeti was staring at him in the same way a cat scrutinizes a mouse at dinner time. It rose to its full height and growled.

'What now, sir?' said Sam, his voice trembling.

'Now we run!' instructed Fearbeard, dropping

the cloth sack and turning to race back down
the hill.

Sam turned and fled too. He could hear the
yeti's stomping footsteps right behind him. The
earth seemed to shake with every step. Sam caught
up with Fearbeard; they were both out of breath.

'See?' said Fearbeard, panting all the while.
'He's doing all the work for us! We'll have him
back to the balloon in no time!'

'What then?' asked Sam.

Before Fearbeard had time to answer, the yeti
roared and Sam and the Captain raced a little
faster down the plateau.

Chapter 4
A slippery escape

Fearbeard and Sam raced from the yeti as fast as their legs could carry them. Sam stole a glance over his shoulder and the galloping creature shook an angry fist. Sam knew how it felt – if he'd been having a nice nap and someone pelted him with snowballs, he'd be pretty angry too!

'This is perfect!' said Fearbeard as they ran.

'Perfect?' spluttered Sam in disbelief. 'What's perfect about this?'

'The yeti is going to chase us all the way back to the balloon,' explained Fearbeard.

'What if he catches us and eats us before we get

there?' said Sam, doing his best to keep up.

'Listen to you, Mr Gloomy Trousers!' said Fearbeard, picking up a little speed. 'I defeated the wailing wasps of Wassamanga, the rabid rats of Rassapotania and the shaggy shepherds of Shepton Mallet. This yeti doesn't worry me!'

'Well, he worries me!' admitted Sam, casting a furtive look back towards the advancing yeti.

The Captain and his cabin boy charged through the thick snow and behind them the yeti matched them step for step. It had been a bit slow and sleepy after the snowballs, but now it was wide awake and ready for a fight. Sam and Fearbeard darted past a boulder and on down the mountainside.

'We're nearly there!' said Fearbeard, pointing to the hot-air balloon.

'So's the yeti!' gulped Sam. He could feel the yeti's warm breath on the back of his neck.

Fearbeard looked behind him and the colour drained from his face. 'Ooerr!' he said when he saw how close the yeti was. 'Give me a shaggy shepherd any day!'

The yeti swiped at them both and Sam jumped out of the way, dodging its massive paw. He lost his footing on the slippery ice and fell face first onto the hard ground. The yeti growled and advanced slowly towards him. Sam closed his eyes. This was it! He was about to become a yeti snack. But instead of feeling the yeti's sharp merciless claws, Sam felt himself sliding. He opened his eyes and found that he was careering face first down the ice sheet like a human toboggan. The yeti blinked and watched him go.

'Great idea!' shouted Fearbeard, jumping onto his tummy and beginning to slide. 'I was just about to suggest it!'

They skidded down the ice towards the hot-air balloon, leaving the yeti far behind.

'Weeeee!' giggled Fearbeard. 'We'll be home for tea and treasure after all!'

It didn't take long
for the yeti to give
chase once again,
but Fearbeard and
Sam had put enough

ground between them that it wasn't an immediate threat.

When they reached the bottom of the hill they skidded to a halt, picked themselves up and dusted off the snow.

'Isn't adventuring fun!' laughed Fearbeard, scurrying towards the balloon.

The yeti was halfway down the slope and getting closer by the second. It didn't look happy.

Fearbeard hopped into the wicker basket and pulled Sam in after him. The balloon was tied to a rock by a thick rope. Fearbeard tried to untie it but his fingers were frozen stiff.

'I don't want to hurry you, Captain,' said Sam, looking at the advancing yeti, 'but we haven't much time!'

'Don't you have your penknife, Sam?' Fearbeard asked, spitting out bits of shredded rope.

'I threw it overboard, sir!' said Sam.

'Well, that was a jolly silly thing to do, wasn't it?' snapped Fearbeard, hands on hips.

Sam was about to argue that it was Fearbeard who had told him to throw it away in the first place when his thoughts were interrupted by the growl of the yeti, now just metres away.

Sam rushed to help Fearbeard with the rope. With his smaller fingers he managed to work the knot loose. Sam unwound the rope from the boulder. There was no time to reel it in and as the balloon began to rise, the rope dangled like a tail from the basket. The yeti watched the balloon rise and roared in frustration.

'Ha!' laughed Fearbeard, blowing a raspberry at the yeti. 'Not so scary now, are we?'

The yeti leapt into the air and grabbed the loose end of the rope, swinging from side to side like a hairy Tarzan. The balloon lurched under the weight and Sam and Fearbeard held on for dear life.

'This keeps getting better and better!' said Fearbeard with a grin. 'I thought we would have to leave him behind, but now we can fly him all the way to the ship!'

Captain Fearbeard munched happily on a custard cream while Sam peered over the edge of the basket. The startled yeti was clinging on with its sharp claws as they sailed over the icy ground. Then Sam remembered the mountain peak. If they had been struggling to clear it with just the two  of them then the yeti's extra weight meant they were certain to crash.

'Sir!' said Sam, nudging Fearbeard's back.

'Not now, Sam!' snapped Fearbeard. 'Let the Captain enjoy his custard cream in peace!'

'But sir!' insisted Sam, pointing towards the fast-approaching mountain.

Fearbeard spat out his biscuit in surprise when he saw the trouble they were in. 'Crumbs!' he said.

'My thoughts exactly!' said Sam, brushing bits of biscuit from his shoulder.

'I'm not talking about your top, Sam!' snapped Fearbeard. 'We need to chuck something overboard and fast!'

Sam rummaged in his pocket for the last thing he had left – his trusty pea-shooter. He was about to throw it over the side when he had an idea. He searched in the Captain's trunk.

'This is no time for fun and games, Sam!' said the Captain. 'Throw it overboard!'

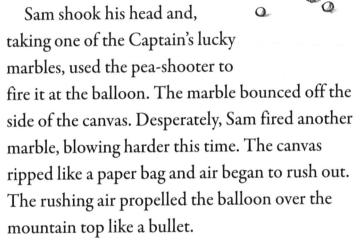

Sam shook his head and, taking one of the Captain's lucky marbles, used the pea-shooter to fire it at the balloon. The marble bounced off the side of the canvas. Desperately, Sam fired another marble, blowing harder this time. The canvas ripped like a paper bag and air began to rush out. The rushing air propelled the balloon over the mountain top like a bullet.

Fearbeard, Sam and the yeti clung on for dear life as the rapidly deflating balloon shot across the sky.

Chapter 5
What goes up ...

The hot-air balloon zoomed through the clouds as air rushed from the hole in its side. Fearbeard and Sam gripped the wicker basket until their knuckles were white. Beneath them, the yeti swung back and forth like a furry yo-yo. Up ahead, the HMS *Albatross* came into view.

'Very good, Sam!' said Captain Fearbeard. 'You can slow us down now.'

'Slow us down?' said Sam as the air hissed out of the balloon. 'I don't think I can!'

'You don't think you can!' roared Fearbeard. 'Then how do you propose we stop?'

'I didn't think of that,' admitted Sam. 'I was just trying to stop us crashing into the mountain!'

The yeti roared as he was pulled through a snowdrift. When the rope came out of the other side, the yeti was nowhere to be seen.

'That is just perfect!' yelled Fearbeard. 'We're on a runaway balloon and now we've lost our yeti!'

Sam had never seen Fearbeard so angry. It was only a matter of time before the air ran out of the balloon and the basket plummeted to the ground.

Sam did his best to stand up for himself. 'With the greatest respect, sir,' he said. 'I saved us from being eaten by a yeti and not long ago you were proposing to throw me overboard!'

'I wish I had now!' shouted Fearbeard, shaking a furious fist at Sam. 'At least I wouldn't be hurtling through the sky like a balloony meteorite!'

As the last of the air escaped from the hole in the balloon, the basket began to fall. Sam braced himself against the wicker.

'We're going to crash, sir!' he cried. 'Hold on tight!'

Fearbeard turned to Sam, eyes blazing. 'I'm the Captain here!' he shouted. 'If anyone is going to tell anyone to hold onto anything then it's ... '

Before Fearbeard could finish his sentence the basket crashed into the ground and skidded across the ice. Sam held on tight as the basket hit a rock, tilted onto its side and Fearbeard was catapulted out like a cork from a bottle.

'Aaaargh!' he cried as he shot through the air. Sam closed his eyes and winced as Fearbeard disappeared into a bank of snow.

When the basket came to rest, Sam picked up his rucksack and checked himself for broken bones. He was a little battered and bruised, but apart from that everything was fine. On the horizon he could see HMS *Albatross* bobbing on the icy waves. At least they didn't have far to go.

Sam ran to the bank where a Captain-shaped splat mark was etched into the snow. He peered into the hole.

'Are you all right in there, Captain?' he asked tentatively.

The roar that came from the snow bank was unlike anything Sam had heard before. If Fearbeard had been angry in the basket, now he was livid.

Fearbeard pulled himself out of the drift. When he emerged he was covered from head to toe in snow, like some kind of abominable snowman. 'Wait until I get my hands on you!' he bellowed, his face and beard covered in ice.

Sam turned and ran for the ship. Fearbeard gave chase, arms outstretched.

Back on the ship, John Pilchard, the ship's first mate, and Pat Leotard, the chief rigging climber, were waiting expectantly for Sam and Captain Fearbeard's return.

John took the telescope from his eye and pointed into the distance. 'Does that look like Sam to you?' he asked.

Pat took the telescope and nodded. 'But where's Fearbeard?' he asked. 'And what's that chasing Sam?'

John took the telescope and looked. The snow-covered creature that was chasing Sam bore no resemblance to the Captain they knew and loved.

'That,' said John, nodding sagely, 'is a yeti.'

'It must have eaten Fearbeard!' gasped Pat.

65

'And now it wants Sam for dessert!'

'Don't worry,' grunted John. 'We'll be waiting for it!'

While John and Pat assembled the rest of the crew, Sam charged across the ice as fast as his legs would carry him. He was now within touching distance of the *Albatross*. Chef McStain lowered the gangplank and Sam ran straight for it. Behind him Captain Fearbeard growled in anger.

'That's it, m'boy,' encouraged the ship's cook. 'You go and hide. We'll see how this yeti likes dealing with someone its own size.'

Sam scampered up the gangplank and into the Captain's quarters. When the snow-covered Captain set foot on the gangplank, all four of the crew jumped on the other end.

'Oh no you don't!' shouted midshipman Trevor Bunion.

The combined weight of the crew made the gangplank act like a see-saw and Fearbeard was catapulted through the air and into the hold. Once he was inside John Pilchard closed the doors and Fearbeard was trapped.

Chef McStain called Sam onto the deck. 'What happened to Fearbeard?' he asked.

Sam didn't know where to begin and stared dumbly at the crew.

'He's too scared to talk,' said Trevor Bunion, ushering Sam towards the kitchen. 'A nice cup of hot chocolate might help.'

As Sam sipped his hot chocolate he listened to the enraged bellowing of the Captain from the hold.

'That yeti's got a temper!' said Chef McStain, rolling his eyes.

Sam sprinkled marshmallows onto his hot chocolate and smiled. He'd tell the crew exactly who was in the hold soon enough. He just needed Fearbeard to calm down a bit first.

Chapter 6
Captain Fearbeard cools off

It took two hours and five packets of custard creams before Fearbeard thawed out and calmed down enough to be let out of the hold. It took another two hours and another five packets for him to forgive Sam for what had happened. In the end they admitted that they had both been at fault. Fearbeard promised never to threaten to throw Sam out of a hot-air balloon again if Sam promised never to fling him into a snowdrift.

The two friends shook hands and stood on the bow of the ship watching the sun set behind an iceberg.

'That yeti was snow joke!' giggled Fearbeard. '*Snow* joke! Get it?'

Sam chuckled obediently as the *Albatross* glided through the deep blue water.

'Onward to adventure, Sam!' said Fearbeard. 'Who knows what daring deeds and brave escapades we will face next time.'

'Must there be a next time, Captain?' asked Sam.

'Invariably!' crowed Fearbeard with a grin. 'Invariably!'

HMS *Albatross* and her crew floated through the Arctic towards adventures new, leaving the yeti far behind and Fearbeard and Sam arguing over whose turn it was to de-gunk the mangle.

Captain Fearbeard and the Boomerang Bang-a-Bang!

Chapter 1
Down on their luck down under

Captain Fearbeard made his excuses to the tribe of Aborigines and ushered Sam out of the village. The sun was baking the arid dusty ground and Fearbeard's bushy beard wilted in the heat as they walked. Once they were safely out of the village Fearbeard turned and gave the tribesmen a polite wave.

'What a complete waste of time,' he muttered out of the corner of his mouth. 'We come all the way to Australia in search of undiscovered creatures and we return with nothing!'

Fearbeard stopped waving as he and Sam turned to begin the long, hot walk back to HMS *Albatross* and the Captain's loyal crew.

'Some explorers come to Australia and discover all sorts of things,' continued Fearbeard. 'Killer spiders, poisonous frogs, the duck-billed platypus! I thought it would be easy!'

Sam rummaged in his backpack and produced a sandwich. While he nibbled, Fearbeard ranted on. 'But oh no!' he complained sarcastically. 'Not for Captain Fearbeard.'

Fearbeard studied the horizon and punched his fist in frustration. 'There's adventure out there somewhere, Sam!' he said. 'I can smell it!'

'I think that might be my lunch, sir,' said Sam apologetically. 'Toasted tripe today. It's not all bad, sir. They did give us this.'

Sam produced the boomerang that the generous Aborigine tribesman had given them as they were leaving.

Fearbeard dismissed it with a shrug. 'A bent stick!' he snorted. 'Rubbish! Almost as bad as that bouncy thing those inventors in America gave us – what was it called?'

'A pogo stick, Captain,' said Sam.

'A pogo stick,' said Fearbeard, shaking his head in disbelief. 'Useless!'

Captain Fearbeard had had high hopes for his trip to Australia and that only served to make his disappointment at returning empty-handed even more acute. Rumour had it that the wild country was full of undiscovered marvels. If that was the case then they were to remain that way – undiscovered. Their time in Australia was at an end and it was time to begin the long voyage home.

'I'm Captain Fearbeard,' grumbled the Captain as they walked. 'I discovered the quacking koalas of Kuala Lumpur, the dancing ducks of Dakar and the marauding magpies of Moreton-in-Marsh! People expect things. Triumphant things!

A bent stick is not a triumphant thing! It's silly!'

'It's called a boomerang, sir,' explained Sam patiently.

'See!' spluttered Fearbeard. 'It's even got a silly name!'

On the horizon Sam could see the crew of the *Albatross* preparing her for the journey home. As they got closer Sam made out Trevor Bunion and Pat Leotard loading barrels of provisions into the hold while John Pilchard made last-minute repairs to the sails.

'They'd better have enough custard creams for the voyage,' said Fearbeard. 'Speaking of which, I might just have one now. To cheer myself up, you understand.'

Sam put the boomerang on the floor and searched in his rucksack for the Captain's emergency packet of biscuits.

While he munched, the Captain picked up the boomerang and examined it again. 'A stick of all things!' he muttered. 'What do they think I am? A puppy? Fetch!'

Fearbeard threw the boomerang away in disgust

then turned to continue the walk back to the ship.

As the boomerang spun through the air it turned 180 degrees and flew straight back towards the Captain, knocking him on the back of the head and clattering him to the floor.

'What do you think of the boomerang now, sir?' asked Sam as he helped the Captain to his feet.

'Truth be told, m'lad,' growled the Captain, 'I'm starting to like it even less.'

Chapter 2
A killer kangaroo

Fearbeard glowered angrily at the boomerang and rubbed the lump that was growing on the back of his head.

'Well that just takes the biscuit!' he said. 'You can't even throw the thing away without it coming back! Let's try that again.'

Fearbeard lifted the boomerang high above his head and threw it into the distance with a loud grunt.

Sam and Fearbeard watched the boomerang disappear into the clear blue sky.

'That should do it!' said Fearbeard, dusting his hands in satisfaction.

Sam wasn't so sure, and while Fearbeard turned to double-check that preparations for the ship's departure were properly underway, Sam kept an eye on the horizon. Sure enough, after a moment, he saw the boomerang hurtling back towards them.

'Out of the way, sir!' said Sam, shoulder-barging

Fearbeard to the floor as the boomerang sailed past.

Fearbeard's fall squashed a tray of iced buns that were waiting to be loaded into the ship's hold and the Captain was furious. 'Have you gone mad?' he said, picking glacé cherries off his uniform and popping them into his mouth. 'Chef's going to kill us for that! I'll make sure he does you first so I can watch!'

'Sorry, sir,' said Sam. 'I was trying to save you another boomerang bonk! It came back again.' Sam held up the boomerang for Fearbeard to see.

'Preposterous!' spluttered the Captain, snatching the boomerang out of Sam's hands. 'What does it take to get rid of this thing?'

Fearbeard lifted the boomerang behind his head again, took a long run-up and heaved it into the sky. Sam crouched behind a barrel, expecting the boomerang back any second, while Fearbeard stood with his hands on his hips and watched it disappear into the bush. When the boomerang didn't return he turned to Sam and grinned.

'I think that's got rid of that!' he announced

smugly. 'Now pick up those squished cakes – you've got some explaining to do!'

Sam dutifully picked up the tray of battered buns and walked towards the gangplank. He was about to get on board the ship when the ground beneath him began to shake.

'Earthquake!' announced Fearbeard, running for cover.

'I don't think so, sir,' said Sam. The shaking was too regular and rhythmic to be an earthquake. An earthquake came once and then it was gone – this shaking was coming every other second and what was more, it was accompanied by a strange thumping sound. Sam turned to see if he could find the source and dropped the tray of buns in surprise when he saw what was coming towards them.

'Now look what you've done!' snapped Fearbeard. 'Clumsy boy!'

Instead of arguing, Sam merely pointed over the Captain's shoulder. Fearbeard turned and blinked in disbelief. Bouncing towards them was the biggest kangaroo either of them had ever seen, and sticking out of its ear was a boomerang.

'Gracious!' said Fearbeard. 'A king-sized kangaroo! This could be the answer to our prayers. It might not be a duck-billed platypus but at least I've discovered something. Fearbeard does it again!'

While Fearbeard beamed with satisfaction, the kangaroo bounded towards them. It was twice as big as Fearbeard and had massive long feet.

'It doesn't look happy, sir,' said Sam.

'I'll say,' agreed Fearbeard. 'It looks hopping mad! *Hopping* mad! Get it?'

Sam did indeed get it, but he wasn't sure this was the right time for jokes. 'I don't think it liked being smacked with your boomerang, sir!' he said.

'Maybe not,' said Fearbeard with a nod. 'But let's not jump to conclusions. *Jump* to conclusions! Get it? Gosh, I'm good!'

Fearbeard slapped his thigh as he collapsed into giggles. By the time he had recovered, the kangaroo was towering over them both.

'It's magnificent,' said Fearbeard, craning his neck to take in the full majesty of the beast. 'If we can get this on the ship and back to London my reputation will be restored!'

Sam couldn't believe his ears. Fearbeard wanted to take this kangaroo back with them? 'I'm not sure that's a good idea, sir!' he said.

'Nonsense,' said Fearbeard, dismissing his cabin boy with a wave of his hand. 'I have a way with animals, just you wait and see!'

Fearbeard took a step towards the furious kangaroo and gave the creature a smart bow. 'Captain Fearbeard at your service,' he announced with a flourish.

The kangaroo glared at the Captain while Sam hid his face behind his hands.

'I appear to have hit you with a boomerang,' chuckled Fearbeard. 'May I?'

Without waiting for a reply, Fearbeard jumped nimbly into the air and plucked the boomerang from the kangaroo's ear. The kangaroo growled angrily.

'How would you like to come to London, old girl?' asked Fearbeard, passing the boomerang to Sam. 'You could have tea with the Queen – I'm sure she'd love to meet you.'

The kangaroo, who'd had quite enough of Fearbeard, stretched out a paw and bopped him on the nose.

'You scoundrel!' shouted Fearbeard, clutching his face. 'I was just trying to be polite!'

Sam tugged gently at Fearbeard's coat. 'Perhaps we should get on board, sir?'

Fearbeard pushed him away. 'Nobody hits Captain Fearbeard and gets away with it, Sam!' he snapped.

Fearbeard turned to the kangaroo and raised his arms like a boxer. 'Come on then, Madam kangaroo,' he taunted. 'Show us what you've got!'

The kangaroo lifted a paw and bopped Fearbeard's nose again.

'Lucky shot!' said Fearbeard.

The kangaroo bopped him on the head.

'I wasn't ready!' protested Fearbeard.

The kangaroo gave Fearbeard another mighty bop on the ear.

'Refereeeeee!' slurred Fearbeard as he fell into a daze. The Captain wobbled back and forth and Sam rushed to try and catch him. Before he could get close, Fearbeard closed his eyes, fainted and tumbled head first

into the giant kangaroo's cavernous front pouch! The kangaroo then turned and hopped back towards the bushes, taking the unconscious Captain with her and leaving Sam holding nothing but a boomerang.

Chapter 3
Kangaroo kidnap

It took a moment for Sam to realize what had happened, but when he did, he sprang into action.

'Stop!' he shouted as the kangaroo bounced towards the bush. The jiggling had obviously revived the Captain and Sam could hear him wailing from inside the pouch.

As Sam watched, the Captain stuck his head out and waved desperately at him. 'Help!' he spluttered. 'I've been kidnapped by a kangaroo!'

Sam gave chase, but it was no use. The kangaroo was bouncing far too fast. Soon she had disappeared into the bush and the Captain's cries were lost to the sound of the wind and waves.

Sam knew that he had to do something. He turned and ran back towards the HMS *Albatross* and her faithful crew for help. He found them relaxing by the seashore, their chores finished and ready to leave. They had been too engrossed in their hard work to notice what had happened to the Captain.

'Captain! Kangaroo! Catastrophe!' blurted Sam as he screeched to a halt in the sand.

Trevor Bunion, the ship's trusty midshipman, gave Sam a curious look. 'Who's Captain Kangaroo when he's at home?' he asked, scratching his chin.

Sam shook his head and started again. 'No!' he shouted, desperate to explain. 'Boomerang! Bang-a-bang!'

The crew looked at each other in confusion. Pat Leotard rose to his feet and put an arm around Sam's shoulder. 'Slow down, lad!' he said. 'Take a deep breath and start at the beginning.'

Sam gulped down lungfuls of air and, when he had collected himself, told the crew what had happened. He told them about the boomerang and how the Captain's efforts to throw it away had angered a king-sized kangaroo. When he reached this bit in his story the crew rolled their eyes.

'Here we go again,' muttered Chef McStain wearily.

'There's always something,' nodded John Pilchard.

'Why can it never be *easy*?' asked Trevor Bunion with an exasperated sigh.

'So what are we going to do?' asked Sam. 'We have to rescue him!'

The crew exchanged a curious look.

'Do we?' said Pilchard.

'Of course we do!' insisted Sam. 'He's the Captain!'

The crew stood and walked up the gangplank towards the *Albatross*.

'Where are you going?' asked Sam. 'Fearbeard went that way!' He pointed towards the bush.

'The thing is,' said Pilchard, leaning over the side of the ship. 'The crew and I have been talking. Frankly, I could sail this ship better than him.'

'You already do,' agreed Chef McStain. 'And if we left without him now there'd be more food for the rest of us on the voyage home!'

Sam couldn't believe his ears ... but the crew hadn't finished.

'His voyages always end in disaster,' said Trevor Bunion. 'I'm thinking of giving up this exploring lark anyway. I fancy becoming an optician – I hear it's all the rage.'

'What we're saying, Sam,' said Leotard, 'is would it be all that bad if Fearbeard didn't come back with us? No more calamity ... '

'No more chaos ... ' agreed Pilchard.

'No more custard creams ... ' said Trevor with a knowing nod.

'You'd leave him here?' spluttered Sam in disbelief. 'After all we've been through? After all he's done for you? After all the adventures we've shared?'

The crew nodded as one.

'That's about the size of it!' said Pilchard, heading for the ship's wheel and barking instructions to the others. 'Hoist the mainsail! Man the rigging!'

The crew jumped to their jobs.

'So are you coming or not?' asked Bunion, preparing to lift the gangplank.

Sam was torn. He didn't want to be left behind, but he didn't want to leave Fearbeard behind either.

Suddenly, Pilchard stuck his head out of the bridge porthole. 'Anyone seen the map?' he asked.

Sam smiled. He knew exactly where it was. Fearbeard always kept the map rolled up tight in his inside pocket. And so the map, like Fearbeard, was currently bouncing into the bush, trapped in a kangaroo's pouch. When Sam told Pilchard where the map was, all the colour drained from the first mate's face.

'We'll not get home without a map!' spluttered Pilchard. 'We need the Captain after all!'

'Well, we need his map ... ' corrected Bunion.

Pilchard wasn't listening. 'Get after that

kangaroo,' he snapped at Sam. 'Or we'll be stuck here forever!'

'But how?' asked Sam. 'It was bouncing so hard I couldn't keep up ... '

Sam paused. A thought was trying to form in his mind. What was it? Bounce ... bounce ... bounce ... Of course! The pogo stick! He couldn't catch up on foot, but maybe he could by bouncing.

Sam ran to the ship's hold and rummaged through all of the strange things they'd collected over the years. Pulling aside a pair of Aztec sandals and a Peruvian nose flute, he found what he was looking for – the pogo stick the Americans had given to them on their last adventure.

He ran down the gangplank, jumped onto the pogo stick and hopped off in pursuit of the runaway kangaroo.

Chapter 4

Pogo à go-go

It took a moment for Sam to get his balance on the pogo stick, but soon he was bouncing like a professional. He clung tight as he propelled himself across the baked dusty ground and into the bush.

The kangaroo had quite a head start, but after twenty minutes of breakneck bouncing, Sam saw the silhouette of the kangaroo on the horizon and heard the Captain's plaintive cries for help drifting across the scrubland.

Soon he was within shouting distance of the Captain. 'I'm coming, sir!' he yelled as he bounced.

The Captain looked like a little rag doll in the kangaroo's massive pouch. He was buffeted back and forth with every bounce.

'I thought you'd never get here!' shouted Fearbeard. 'Help me!'

'That's what I'm trying to do,' explained Sam.

Their conversation alerted the kangaroo to

Sam's presence. When she saw Sam on the pogo stick she narrowed her eyes and bounced even faster. Sam did his best to catch up but it was no use. Had he really seen the last of Captain Fearbeard?

As he bounced extra hard over a rock, the boomerang dug into his back. Sam had an idea. *He* might not be able to catch up with the kangaroo, but the boomerang would!

Sam plucked the boomerang from his back pocket and, clinging to the pogo stick one-handed, prepared to throw it at the kangaroo. He didn't want to hurt the animal, but he might be able to slow her down long enough to mount a rescue.

Sam rode the pogo stick like a rodeo cowboy, closed one eye against the glare of the sun and took aim. When he was ready he threw the boomerang as hard as he could at the kangaroo's hopping feet.

The boomerang flew through the air, skimming the ground and slicing through the arid grass that sprung in patches through the bush.

At first Sam was certain that he had missed his

target, but his heart soared as the boomerang bounced off a boulder and clattered into the kangaroo's legs, tripping the mighty beast.

The kangaroo growled and tumbled head over heels. As it fell, Captain Fearbeard was thrown from the pouch. He spun through the air and landed with an 'Oof!' on the dusty ground.

Fearbeard and the kangaroo were both dazed and Sam seized his chance. With the kangaroo lying on the floor, he pogoed his way over to the Captain and tried to revive him. He gave the Captain a slap on the face and Fearbeard's eyes popped open.

'What is the meaning of this?' he spluttered. 'I'll fight you all!'

'It's me, sir,' said Sam as the Captain rose to his feet. 'We need to get out of here!'

Behind them, the kangaroo was starting to come round. 'Grab onto me, Captain,' Sam said. 'And hold on tight! This might be trickier with two!'

The Captain clung onto Sam's back and together they bounced back the way they had come. The combined weight of the Captain and Sam made the pogo stick bounce higher than before and soon they had left the kangaroo for dust.

Undeterred, the kangaroo gave chase. Fearbeard stole a look over his shoulder. 'That's the way, Sam!' he encouraged. 'We'll show that brute who's the real hopping hero around here!'

The kangaroo was still dazed from her fall and tired out from carrying the Captain all the way into the bush, so she wasn't as fast as she had been. It was only when Sam and the Captain neared the ship that the kangaroo found some reserve of strength and began a frantic last hop.

'Quick, Sam!' shouted the Captain. 'She's right behind us!'

Sam gritted his teeth and hopped as if his life depended on it.

The gangplank was still down and the crew

of the *Albatross* were gathered on the deck of
the boat awaiting the Captain's return. When
they saw Sam and Fearbeard hopping towards
them, pursued by a killer kangaroo, they shouted
encouragement.

'Come on!' shouted Pilchard.
'You can do it!'

Sam bounced straight
for the gangplank
and with three
mighty hops he and
Fearbeard were
safely aboard.

The kangaroo was
ready to give chase, but
Trevor Bunion kicked the gangplank into the water
and the kangaroo stood fuming on the shore.

'Hoist the mainsail!' instructed Fearbeard,
jumping off the pogo stick and taking command.

The crew ran to their stations.

'Have you got the map, sir?' asked Pat Leotard.

Fearbeard reached into his pocket and handed
him the treasured parchment.

'I never go anywhere without it!' he said with a grin. 'Let's head for home!'

Sam packed the pogo stick away and was about to do the same with the boomerang when Fearbeard stopped him.

'Perhaps there is a use for that after all!' he said, tucking it into his pocket and heading for his private quarters.

Sam was about to follow him when John Pilchard and the rest of the crew stopped him.

'You know all that stuff earlier?' said Pilchard. 'About leaving the Captain behind?'

Sam nodded.

'We were only joking,' said Trevor Bunion.

Sam gave the crew a suspicious look. 'You seemed quite serious about it to me!' he said.

'Well, we weren't,' said Chef McStain, putting an arm over Sam's shoulder. 'And just to show there's no hard feelings, there'll be double helpings of chocolate pudding for you every night until we reach London town.'

Sam smiled – maybe being an explorer's cabin boy wasn't such a bad job after all.

Chapter 5
Boomerang back-scratcher

Later that night, as the *Albatross* made for open water and the long journey home, a strange sound filled the still night air. 'Ooh! Aaah! That's better!'

It was coming from the Captain's quarters. Sam went to see what the Captain was doing. When he stepped inside he couldn't believe what he saw. The Captain was sitting on his chair, boomerang in hand, using it to scratch his back.

'Told you I'd find a use for this thing somehow,' he said with a smile. 'The best back-scratcher I

ever had! We'll make a fortune when we get back to England. Captain Fearbeard does it again!'

Sam chuckled. He had to admit, for all of his mistakes and flaws, the Captain had a way of coming out all right in the end.

Soon the *Albatross* had left the Australian coast far behind her and Sam and Fearbeard stood at a porthole watching the land disappear.

'Onward to adventure, Sam!' said Fearbeard. 'Who knows what daring deeds and brave escapades we will face next time.'

'Must there be a next time, Captain?' asked Sam.

'Invariably!' crowed Fearbeard with a grin. 'Invariably!'

And with that, HMS *Albatross* and her crew sailed towards the bright lights of London, leaving the kangaroo to its happy hopping and Fearbeard and Sam arguing over whose turn it was to mop behind the toilet.

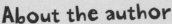
About the author

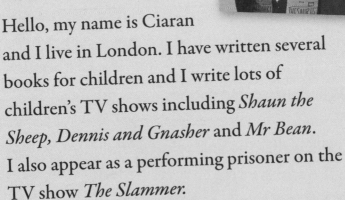

Hello, my name is Ciaran and I live in London. I have written several books for children and I write lots of children's TV shows including *Shaun the Sheep, Dennis and Gnasher* and *Mr Bean.* I also appear as a performing prisoner on the TV show *The Slammer.*

I enjoy creating characters that make children laugh and hope that loveable buffoon Captain Fearbeard is no exception. He might be based on a real person, but I'm not telling you who! If you ever find yourself on a ship with someone like him – jump off!